Alive

The Final Evolution

2

Story by Tadashi Kawashima

Art by Adachitoka

Translated and adapted by

Anastasia Moreno

Lettered by

North Market Street Graphics

Ballantine Books • New York

A Del Rey Trade Paperback Original

Published in the United States by Del Rey Books, an imprint of The Random House Publishing Group, a division of Random House, Inc., New York.

Publication rights arranged through Kodansha Ltd.

First published in Japan in 2003 by Kodansha Ltd., Tokyo

ISBN 978-0-345-49922-6

Printed in the United States of America

www.delreymanga.com

9 8 7 6 5 4 3 2 1

Translator/Adapter—Anastasia Moreno
Lettering—North Market Street Graphics

Contents

Tadashi Kawashima

The story gets better as you read it!
That's *ALIVE*!

Thank you ♡

Adachitoka

It's forever summertime in the manga.
I wish I could draw the characters in winter clothes....

Honorifics Explained

Throughout the Del Rey Manga books, you will find Japanese honorifics left intact in the translations. For those not familiar with how the Japanese use honorifics and, more important, how they differ from American honorifics, we present this brief overview.

Politeness has always been a critical facet of Japanese culture. Ever since the feudal era, when Japan was a highly stratified society, use of honorifics—which can be defined as polite speech that indicates relationship or status—has played an essential role in the Japanese language. When addressing someone in Japanese, an honorific usually takes the form of a suffix attached to one's name (example: "Asuna-san"), is used as a title at the end of one's name, or appears in place of the name itself (example: "Negi-sensei," or simply "Sensei").

Honorifics can be expressions of respect or endearment. In the context of manga and anime, honorifics give insight into the nature of the relationship between characters. Many English translations leave out these important honorifics and therefore distort the feel of the original Japanese. Because Japanese honorifics contain nuances that English honorifics lack, it is our policy at Del Rey not to translate them. Here, instead, is a guide to some of the honorifics you may encounter in Del Rey Manga.

-san: This is the most common honorific and is equivalent to Mr., Miss, Ms., or Mrs. It is the all-purpose honorific and can be used in any situation where politeness is required.

-sama: This is one level higher than "-san" and is used to confer great respect.

-dono: This comes from the word "tono," which means "lord." It is an even higher level than "-sama" and confers utmost respect.

-kun: This suffix is used at the end of boys' names to express familiarity or endearment. It is also sometimes used by men among friends, or when addressing someone younger or of a lower station.

-chan: This is used to express endearment, mostly toward girls. It is also used for little boys, pets, and even among lovers. It gives a sense of childish cuteness.

Bozu: This is an informal way to refer to a boy, similar to the English terms "kid" and "squirt."

Sempai/ Senpai: This title suggests that the addressee is one's senior in a group or organization. It is most often used in a school setting, where underclassmen refer to their upperclassmen as "sempai." It can also be used in the workplace, such as when a newer employee addresses an employee who has seniority in the company.

Kohai: This is the opposite of "sempai" and is used toward underclassmen in school or newcomers in the workplace. It connotes that the addressee is of a lower station.

Sensei: Literally meaning "one who has come before," this title is used for teachers, doctors, or masters of any profession or art.

-[blank]: This is usually forgotten in these lists, but it is perhaps the most significant difference between Japanese and English. The lack of honorific means that the speaker has permission to address the person in a very intimate way. Usually, only family, spouses, or very close friends have this kind of permission. Known as *yobisute,* it can be gratifying when someone who has earned the intimacy starts to call one by one's name without an honorific. But when that intimacy hasn't been earned, it can be very insulting.

Alive

2

Writer/ Tadashi Kawashima
Artist/ Adachitoka

story

Taisuke Kanou lived with his older sister, who had raised him since their parents passed away. He always protected his close friend, Yuichi Hirose, from bullies, and always argued with his childhood girlfriend, Megumi Ochiai. His peaceful, everyday life was shattered when a string of mass suicides occurred around the world during the week dubbed "Nightmare Week."

An illusion of floating in the middle of the universe. A girl jumping to her death, smiling peacefully. The slaughtered bodies of four upperclassmen bullies surrounding Hirose as he denied any wrongdoing. A classmate who looked at the brutally murdered bodies nonchalantly as she jumped to her death. The strange stare of Deputy Inspector Katsumata, who interrogated Hirose as a murder suspect. And Taisuke's encounter with the random murderer, Yura, who considered him to be a "comrade" – Taisuke experienced stranger incidents by the day, but he yearned to go back to his normal life someday.

Taisuke Kanou
High school student weak in fights, but has a strong sense of justice. Both parents died, so he lives alone with his older sister.

Yuichi Hirose
Taisuke's close friend. Has a cute face, but is rather shy, making him an easy target of bullying by upperclassmen.

Megumi Ochiai
Taisuke's childhood girlfriend. She always ends up arguing with Taisuke because she worries about him so much.

Youko Kanou
Taisuke's older sister and also school nurse. Strong-willed woman who raised Taisuke after their parents died.

contents

But his wish was in vain. Hirose, returning to the reopened school, was no longer his old self. He forcefully led Megumi and was over-confident, claiming that he actually killed the upperclassmen bullies. He then tried to kill Taisuke with his newly acquired superhuman powers, but instead, accidentally pushed Megumi off the roof. Taisuke jumped off the roof, trying to save her. There was no way the two could survive that fall, but somehow, they landed safely and stayed alive. Unfortunately, Taisuke was seriously injured from the fall and lost consciousness. Hirose never looked back as he kidnapped Megumi and disappeared...

Takumi Yura
Mysterious man in coveralls with superhuman powers who claims to be a leader of humans, but slaughters people mercilessly.

Shigeki Katsumata
Detective who interrogates Hirose as a murder suspect. Seems to be manipulating Hirose.

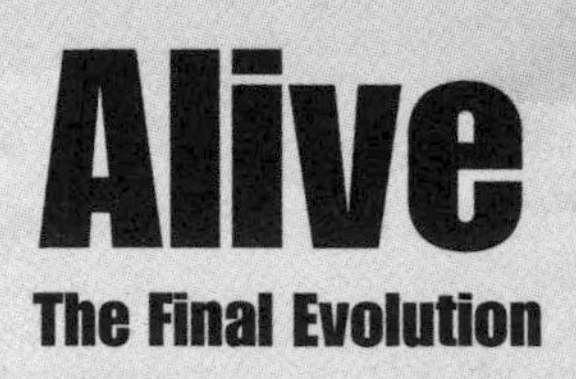
Alive
The Final Evolution

I'M GOING TO MY "COMRADES."
GOODBYE.

Mr. Taisuke Kanou
WAIT...

Chapter 4
Any Normal Human Would Normally...
I don't want to go home in the dark.

CRUSH
YOU...!

DRIP
DRIP
IDIOT!!

YOU WERE UNCONSCIOUS FOR THREE DAYS!
THIS AIN'T NO TIME TO SLEEP!!

THREE DAYS...
ROAR

SPAK
ROAR
!
MEGU...!

MEGU! WHERE IS MEGU?!
AND HIRO?!

TELL ME, SIS!
......

BOTH OF THEM...
ARE MISSING.

......

シャ….
SHHHT...

READ THIS.

RECOGNIZE THIS POLICE STATION?
IT'S WHERE HIROSE-KUN WAS TAKEN INTO CUSTODY.
THREE DAYS AGO, THERE WERE BRUTAL MURDERS THERE.
Police Station Slaughter
56 Employees Dead
Connection to Boy H?
At five o'clock on the 12th, a college student (21) discovered several police station employees lying down at the front information counter of the Tokyo City Nakano-ku Central Police Station and called 911.
The student entered the police station to renew his license, but instead found an unconscious woman lying on the floor, and sought help in the neighborhood.
The police station was con-
POLICE
POLICE
POLICE

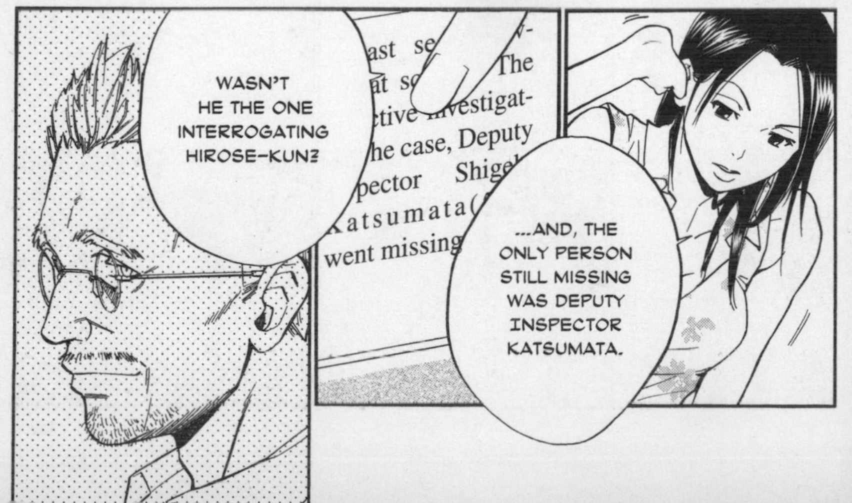
...AND, THE ONLY PERSON STILL MISSING WAS DEPUTY INSPECTOR KATSUMATA.
WASN'T HE THE ONE INTERROGATING HIROSE-KUN?
went missing

HIROSE-KUN DISAPPEARED THAT SAME DAY, TOO...
THE POLICE ARE INVESTIGATING POSSIBLE CONNECTIONS BETWEEN THOSE TWO.
High school girl missing
Nakano-ku
of the 12th, the father of a
high school girl (16) called
911 to have the police locate
her whereabouts.
The high school girl attended
the same school as Boy H, and
was witnessed to be with him
earlier on the 12th. They were
also seen at the Central Police

ADD TO THAT YOUR PECULIAR WOUNDS...
YOU GUYS WERE DEFINITELY MIXED UP IN SOMETHING!

THE POLICE ASKED ME ALL SORTS OF QUESTIONS!
I THINK THEY'LL COME ASK YOU, TOO...
JUST WHAT IS GOING ON HERE?
TELL ME!
AH...

Police Stat

56 Employees Dead

Connection to Boy H?

At five o'clock on the 12th, a college student (21) discovered several police station employees lying down at the front information counter of the Tokyo City Nakano-ku Central Police Station and called 911.

The student entered the poli station to renew his licens but instead found an unco scious woman lying on and sought help in

olice
ense,
ncon-

I'M BACK -
THAT IDIOT...!

HE'S GOT A HOLE IN HIS STOMACH!!
WHAT IS HE TRYING TO DO IN THAT CONDITION?!

WHERE'D YOU GO, TAISUKE!

HUFF
HUFF

GOSH!
WHAT THE HECK IS GOING ON?!

ひぃっ
PANT
SOMEONE TELL ME!
JUST WHAT IS GOING ON?!
PANT
ひぃっ

I DEFINITELY FELL OFF THAT ROOF!
SLIP
ANY NORMAL HUMAN WOULD NORMALLY DIE FROM A FALL LIKE THAT.
SO, WHY AM I ALIVE?!
GASP

OH WAIT... MY WOUNDS...
WHY DOESN'T IT HURT...?
IT'S ONLY BEEN THREE DAYS...
PEEL
ANY NORMAL HUMAN
WOULD NORMALLY BE IN PAIN...

WAAAAAAAAAHHH!!

じろじろ
STARE
ひそひそ
WHISPER

はっ
GASP
はぁ
GASP
はぁ
GASP

MEGU'S HOUSE...

THOSE ARE MEGU'S PARENTS...
POLICE

!
MRS. O...

....

WHAT THE HELL AM I DOING...

"HIRO KIDNAPPED MEGU."
I CAN'T SAY THAT TO THEM!
IT'S ALREADY BEEN THREE DAYS!

I NEED TO FIND THEM FIRST!!
RUSTLE

DASH
HIRO'S HOUSE...!
はっ
GASP
はぁっ
GASP
MANAGER!
はっ
HUFF
はっ
HUFF
IS HIRO BACK?!
WHA...TAI-CHAN, WHY ARE YOU DRESSED LIKE THAT!!
Manager's Office
WHERE'S HIRO...
G-CHAK
ガチャ
GET IN HERE!
EH? BUT...
JUST DO IT!!

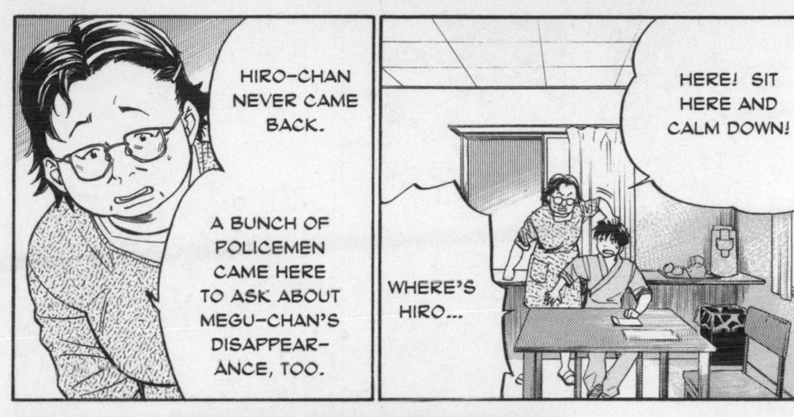
HERE! SIT HERE AND CALM DOWN!
WHERE'S HIRO...
HIRO-CHAN NEVER CAME BACK.
A BUNCH OF POLICEMEN CAME HERE TO ASK ABOUT MEGU-CHAN'S DISAPPEARANCE, TOO.

HIRO-CHAN'S MOTHER RECENTLY DIED, TOO. WHAT IN THE WORLD IS GOING ON...

THE THREE OF YOU USED TO PLAY TOGETHER...
Stupid
TAISUKI WAS HERE
It's actually "Taisuke"
YOU NEED SOME CLOTHES! I'LL GO FIND MY SON'S CLOTHING...
CLENCH

CHANGE INTO THESE!
CLINK

THIS...

1201
KEYS TO HIROSE-SAN'S ROOM.
I THOUGHT YOU MIGHT FIND SOMETHING THERE.

WINK
DON'T TELL THE POLICE, OKAY?

THA...
THANK YOU!!

1201
Hirose
ガチャガチャ
CHK
CHK
ガチャンッ
G-CHAK

ガチャ
SWING

THUMP
THUMP
THUMP
HIRO!
BAM

MEGU!
THUMP
タッタッ
THUMP
ガチャ
G-CHAK
バン
BAM
シャッ
SHHAT
ガチャ
CLICK
ガラッ
SLIDE

TING
TING...

チリ…
TING...
チリン…
TING...

チリ
TING
チリン…
TING...

チリン…
TING...
チリ…
TING...

バタン…
BAM...
キィ
CREAK
……

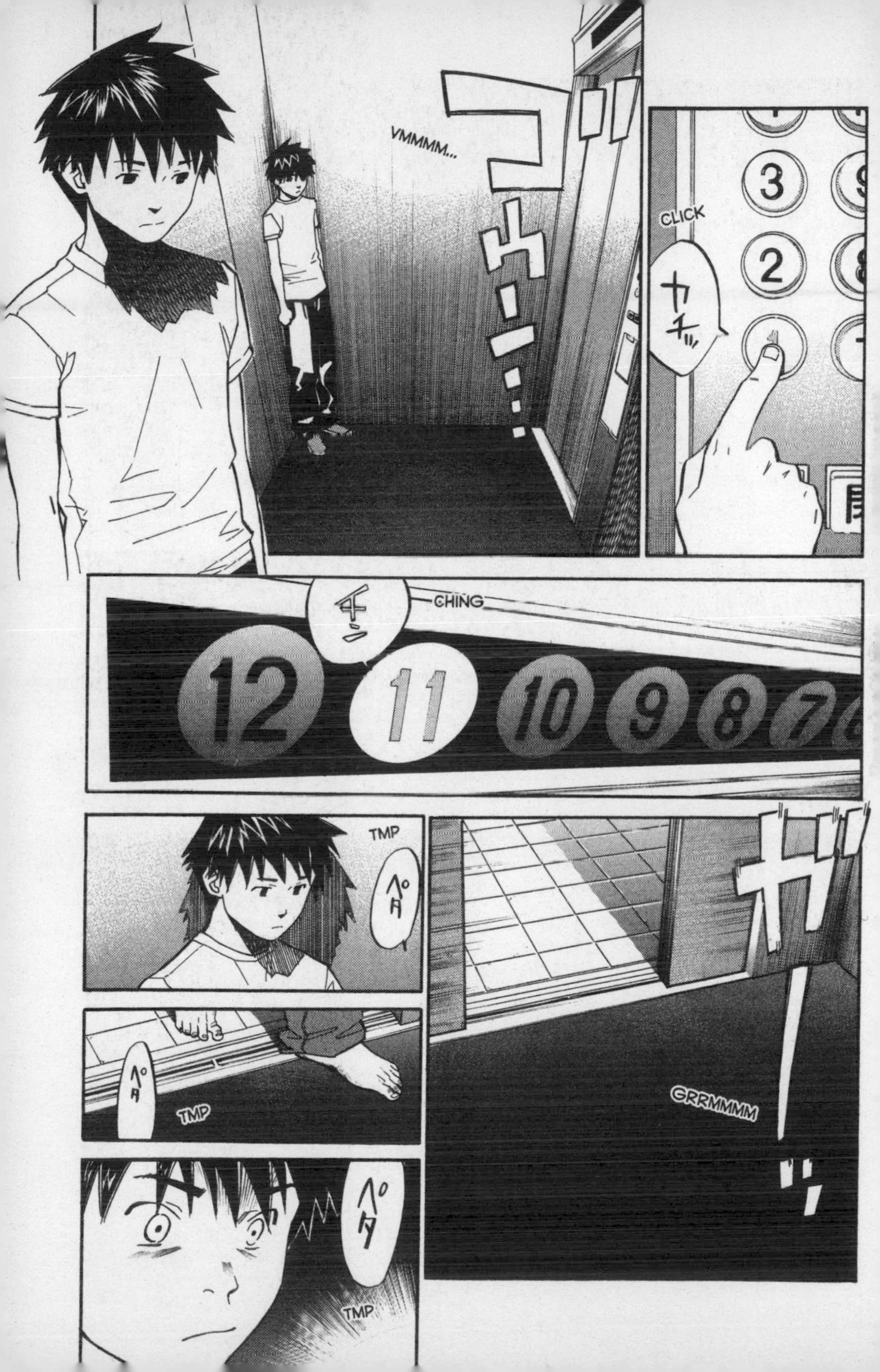

VMMMM...
ゴウン…
CLICK
カチッ
CHING
チン
12
11
10
9
8
TMP
ペタ
ガ
GRRMMMM
ッ
ペタ
TMP
ペタ
TMP

BAM
GRRMMMM

HEY
TAISUKE... RIGHT?

IT'S... HIM...!!

LOOK AT YOU... ACTING LIKE SCUM... HOW PATHETIC.

YOU'RE STILL CLUELESS, AREN'T YOU?
KATTSUN WAS RIGHT...

IN CASE YOU DIDN'T KNOW ALREADY, THIS WORLD IS UNDERGOING A NEW EVOLUTION.
HUMANS ARE NOW
FOSSILS.

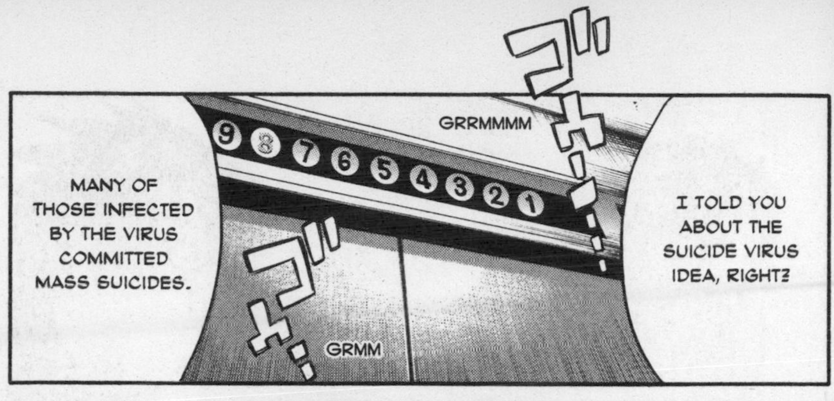
I TOLD YOU ABOUT THE SUICIDE VIRUS IDEA, RIGHT?
GRRMMMM
GRMM
MANY OF THOSE INFECTED BY THE VIRUS COMMITTED MASS SUICIDES.

BUT THOSE FEW THAT WERE INFECTED BUT DIDN'T DIE – "COMRADES" LIKE YOU AND ME...
EVOLVED.

COMPARED TO THOSE THAT DIED AND THE SCUM LEFT OVER...
WE'RE AT A HIGHER LEVEL.

YOU'LL NEED TO ACCEPT THIS FACT!

BUT, IF YOU NEVER EVOLVE...

I'LL JUST KILL YOU.

....!!

GRRMMM
WELL, IT'S BETTER TO HAVE FAIL-URES LIKE YOU AROUND THAN NO ONE AT ALL...
GRRMMM
IT'S JUST TOO BORING WITH JUST THE KID AND THE OLD MAN...
WE'RE GONNA HEAD NORTH.
GRRMMM
WHY DON'T YOU COME WITH US?
THE OLD MAN KATSUMATA WASN'T TOO THRILLED AT THE IDEA, THOUGH.
BRING KANOU-KUN WITH US?
...NOT NOW.
NOT WHILE HIROSE-KUN IS WITH US.

ガーッ
GRRMMM

WAIT... HIROSE? HIROSE IS WITH YOU?!

OF COURSE. HE'S A "COMRADE" TOO.

COMRADE...?
Hah!

WHAT ABOUT MEGU?!
ガッ
GRAB
WHERE IS MEGU?!

OH YEAH, HE BROUGHT SOMEONE ALONG.
SOME CHICK.

WHERE...
NO, TAI-CHAN!

DON'T BE ROUGH ON PEOPLE!
YOU NEED TO BEHAVE YOURSELF...

YOU TOOK SO LONG, SO I WAS WORRIED ABOUT YOU!

YOU'RE HUNGRY, AREN'T YOU? COME EAT DINNER WITH ME.
AH NO...

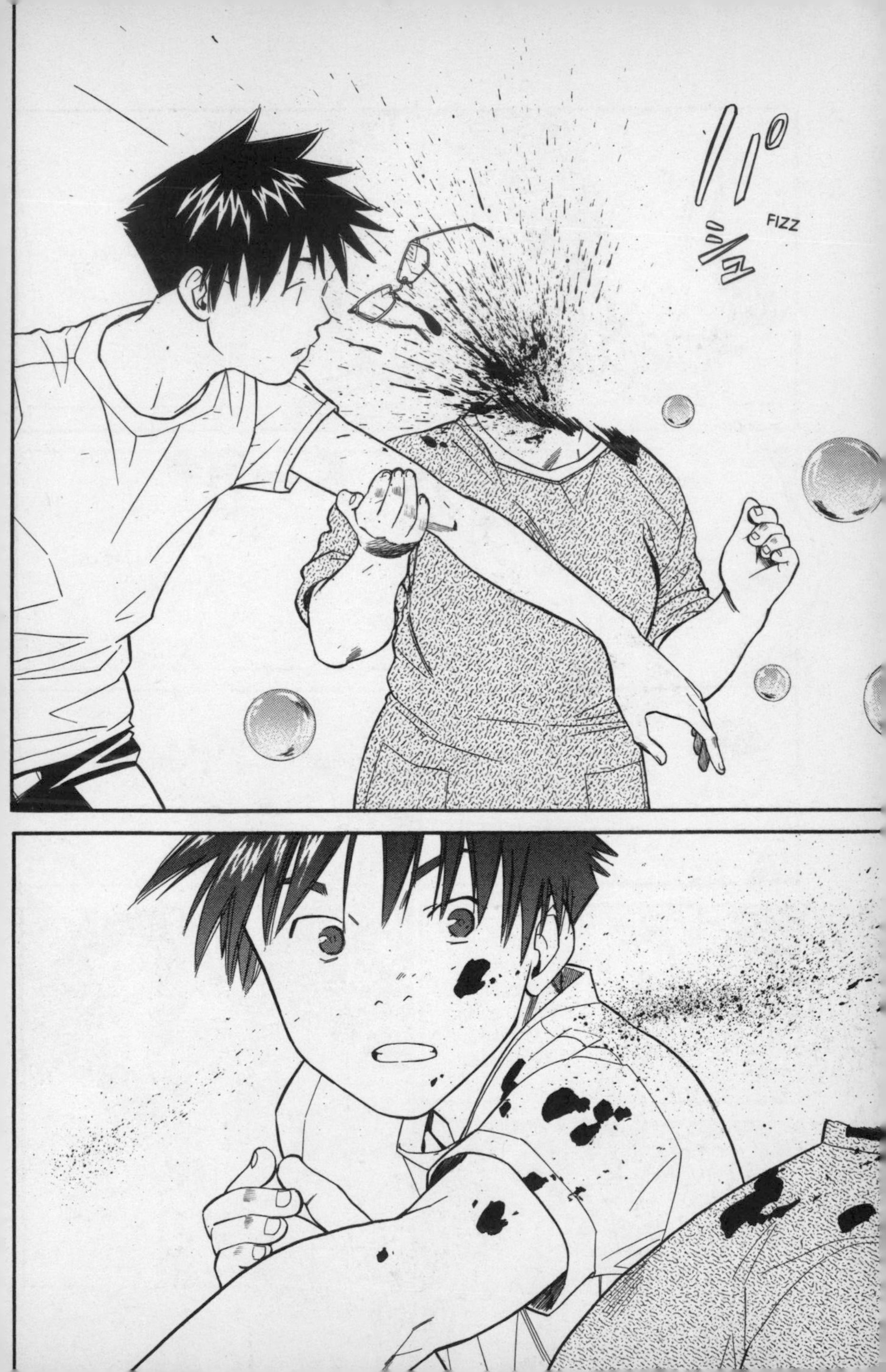
パシュ
FIZZ

FIZZ
POP
AH...

AHH...!

GOOD RIDDANCE...
DAMN SCUM...

LIKE IT? POWERFUL, EH?

THIS LOOKS LIKE A SOAP BUBBLE...
BUT THIS AIN'T NO KID'S TOY, YOU KNOW.

HIGHLY COMPRESSED AIR IS IN THESE BABIES.
SO IF IT BREAKS, BOOM!
IT'S A TINY BOMB.

IT'S UNDER MY COMPLETE CONTROL.
IT WON'T BLOW UNTIL I WANT IT TO.
FLOAT

THIS BEAUTY'S A WASTE TO USE ON SCUM, HUH?

I SUPPOSE THEY SHOULD SPLATTER LIKE A MASTER-PIECE IN THEIR FINAL MOMENT, THOUGH.
OTHERWISE, THEY'LL JUST ROT LIKE THE SCUM THEY ARE.

OH, BUT THEY WON'T LEAVE ANY BONES...
SO I GUESS THEY CAN'T EVEN BE A FOSSIL, HUH?

KYAAAHH!

SIS...
TAISUKE!
YOU'RE COVERED IN...
BLOOD!

!!
DON'T...

ボコ
BLUB
ボボボ
BLU-BLU-BLUB

WHOOF

EH...?!

RUN AWAY!

FIZZLE
シュ....

HURRY...

GRAB

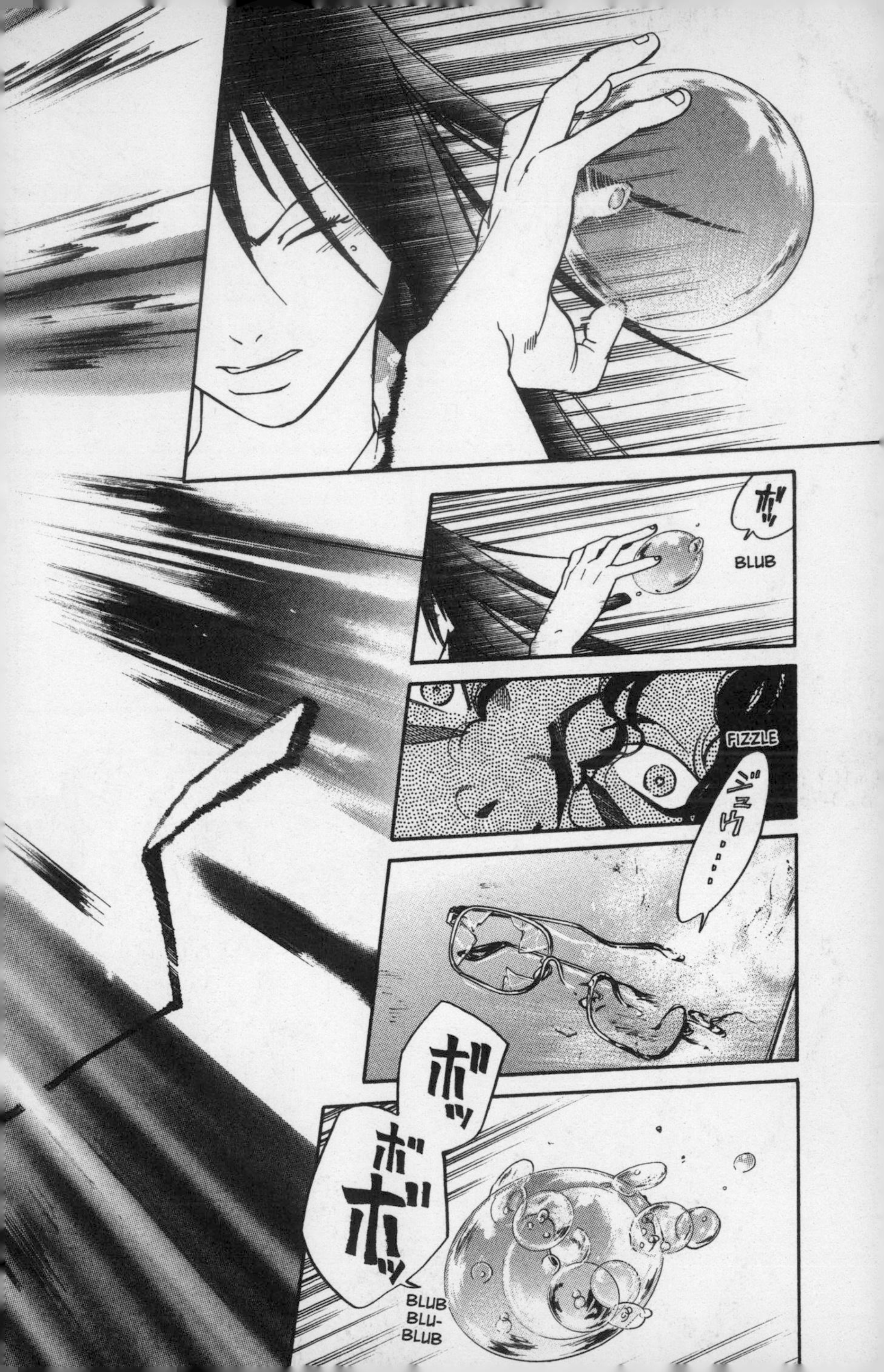
ボッ
BLUB
FIZZLE
ジュウ.....
ボッ
ボッ
ボッ
BLUB
BLU-
BLUB

BOOM

CRUMBLE
CRUMBLE
HACK
COUGH!!
COUGH!

OUCH!
WHAT WAS THAT...?!

AH...

I LET HIM GET AWAY...
I SUCK.
Cough

COMMOTION
...OH WELL.
What's going on?
What happened?
I'M SURE WE'LL MEET AGAIN.

Chapter 4/ End

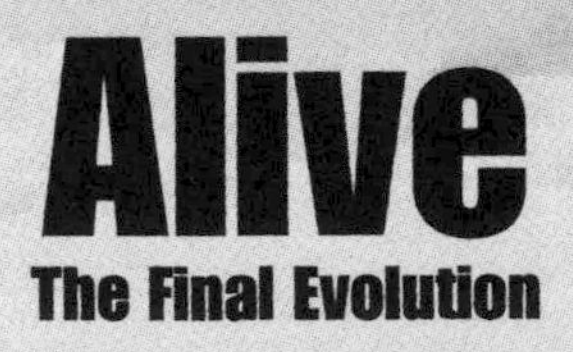
Alive
The Final Evolution

CHIRP
CHIRP
CHIRP
CHIRP
I'LL EXPLAIN EVERYTHING...
TOMORROW...
SORRY TO MAKE YOU WORRIED.
...I DON'T KNOW WHAT HAPPENED TO HIM...
BUT HE'D BETTER TELL ME EVERYTHING TODAY.
GOOD - ...

Chapter 5
I'm Leaving.
What can I do?

?
"TO SIS, I'M..."
To Sis,
I'm leaving for a long while.
Actually, it might not take that long, but...
I'll go look for Megu and
I thought about it last
But I can't imagine
And all this bad stuff
"LEAVING FOR A LONG WHILE..."?
No way...
EH?
TO SIS,
I'M LEAVING FOR A LONG WHILE.
NO WAY...
Mysterious explosion in the
Apartment resident found dead
To Sis,
I'm leaving for a long while.
Actually, it might not take that long, but...

ACTUALLY, IT MIGHT NOT TAKE THAT LONG, BUT...
I'LL GO LOOK FOR MEGU AND HIRO...
CLOMP

I THOUGHT ABOUT IT LAST NIGHT...
He's kidding...
BUT I CAN'T IMAGINE LIFE WITHOUT MEGU AND HIRO...

AND ALL THIS BAD STUFF HAPPENED, LIKE MASS SUICIDES, MYSTERIOUS DEATHS AND YESTERDAY'S EXPLOSION IN THAT APARTMENT...
TROT
IT'S PROBABLY MY FAULT...
MAYBE I'M RELATED TO ALL THIS STUFF.

AT Mansion
POLICE
POLICE
POLICE
POLICE
IT'S PROBABLY MY FAULT THAT SOME PEOPLE DIED.
YOU PROBABLY HAVE NO IDEA WHAT I'M TALKING ABOUT.
HFF
はっ
HFF
はっ
AND ACTUALLY, I REALLY DON'T KNOW EITHER.
BUT
はっ
HFF
ONCE I BRING BACK MEGU AND HIRO, I'LL EXPLAIN IT TO YOU.
はあっ
HFF
UNTIL THEN, PLEASE DON'T WORRY ABOUT ME.
GASP
HOW...!

...SO, I'M LEAVING.
HOW DARE YOU!!

SHE WON'T BUY THAT... FOR SURE...
Sigh
WHRRR
BUT IF I STAY HERE
SIS WILL BE IN DANGER...!
ガッ
STEP

WE'RE HEADING NORTH.
TO THE NORTH...!

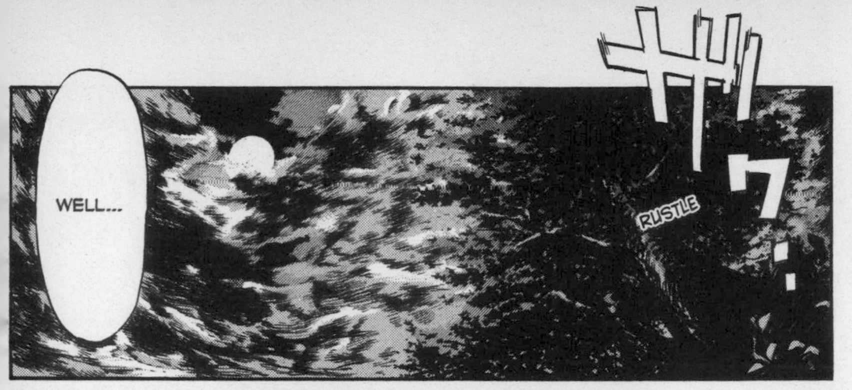
WELL...
RUSTLE

I RODE ALL DAY TOWARD THE NORTH...
BUT WHAT NOW?
MEOW
MEOW

RUMBLE
CLUES...
ROLL
THE ONLY CLUE TO FIND THOSE TWO IS "NORTH"...

THAT GUY SAID DEPUTY INSPECTOR KATSUMATA WAS WITH MEGU AND HIRO.
IF I GO THERE, I MIGHT FIND THEM.

BUT THOSE FEW THAT WERE INFECTED BUT DIDN'T DIE – "COMRADES" LIKE YOU AND ME...
EVOLVED.
WAHAHA. COMRADE! COMRADE!
SLAP
SLAP
WHAT?
HE KEPT REFERRING TO A "COMRADE." WHAT DOES HE MEAN BY THAT?

I'M GOING TO MY "COMRADES."
EVEN HIRO SAID THAT.
OF COURSE. HE'S A "COMRADE" TOO.
HIRO, THAT GUY, AND KATSUMATA ARE "COMRADES"?
I HAVE SPECIAL POWERS NOW!

OH... SO YOU WERE A "COMRADE" TOO, KANOU-KUN...

SIT UP
"COM-RADE," TOO, KANOU-KUN...

ME TOO...?

I'M FINE, EVEN AFTER I FELL FROM THAT ROOF.
SLIP

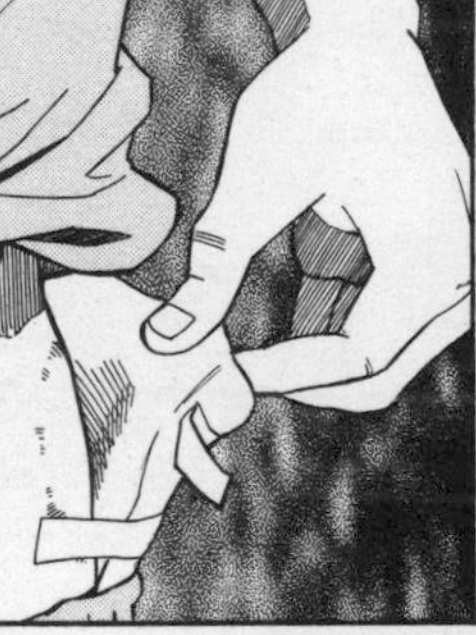
ALSO, MY STOMACH WOUND HEALED TOO QUICKLY.

AND LAST NIGHT...
GRAB
HOW WAS I ABLE TO BLOCK IT!?

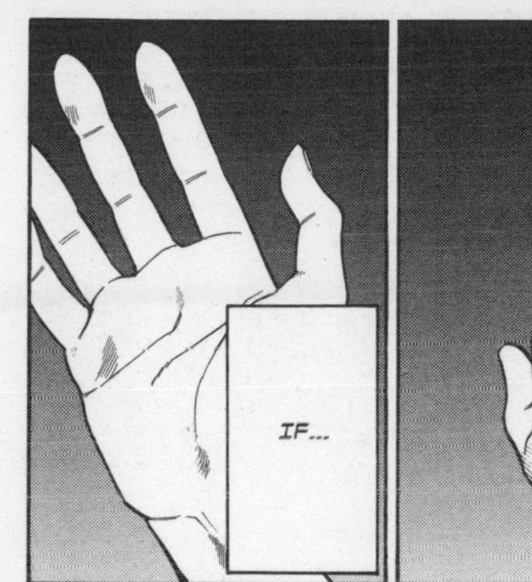
IF...

IF I'M A "COMRADE" LIKE THEY SAY...

I ALSO HAVE "POWERS"...
THEN I...

WHAT AM I DOING...?
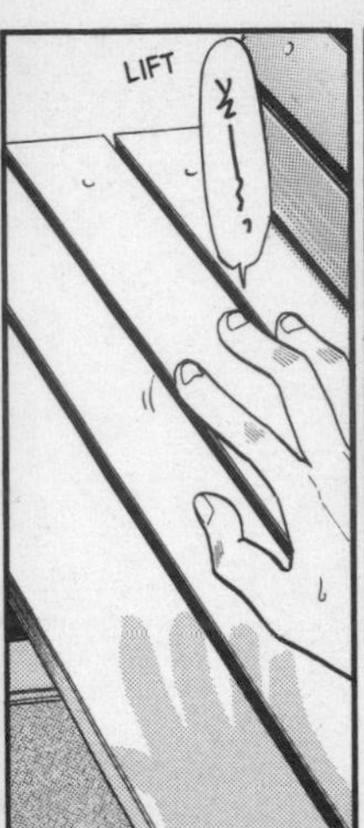
LIFT

ARRGHH!

OH CRAP!
TRICKLE
TRICKLE

A- ANYWAY!
CLINK CLINK
I JUST NEED TO GO NORTH...

WHRRRL

NO! I NEED TO SOLVE THIS!
BUT WHAT CAN I DO?!

DRIZZLE

FIZZ
FIZZ

シュウ…
FIZZLE

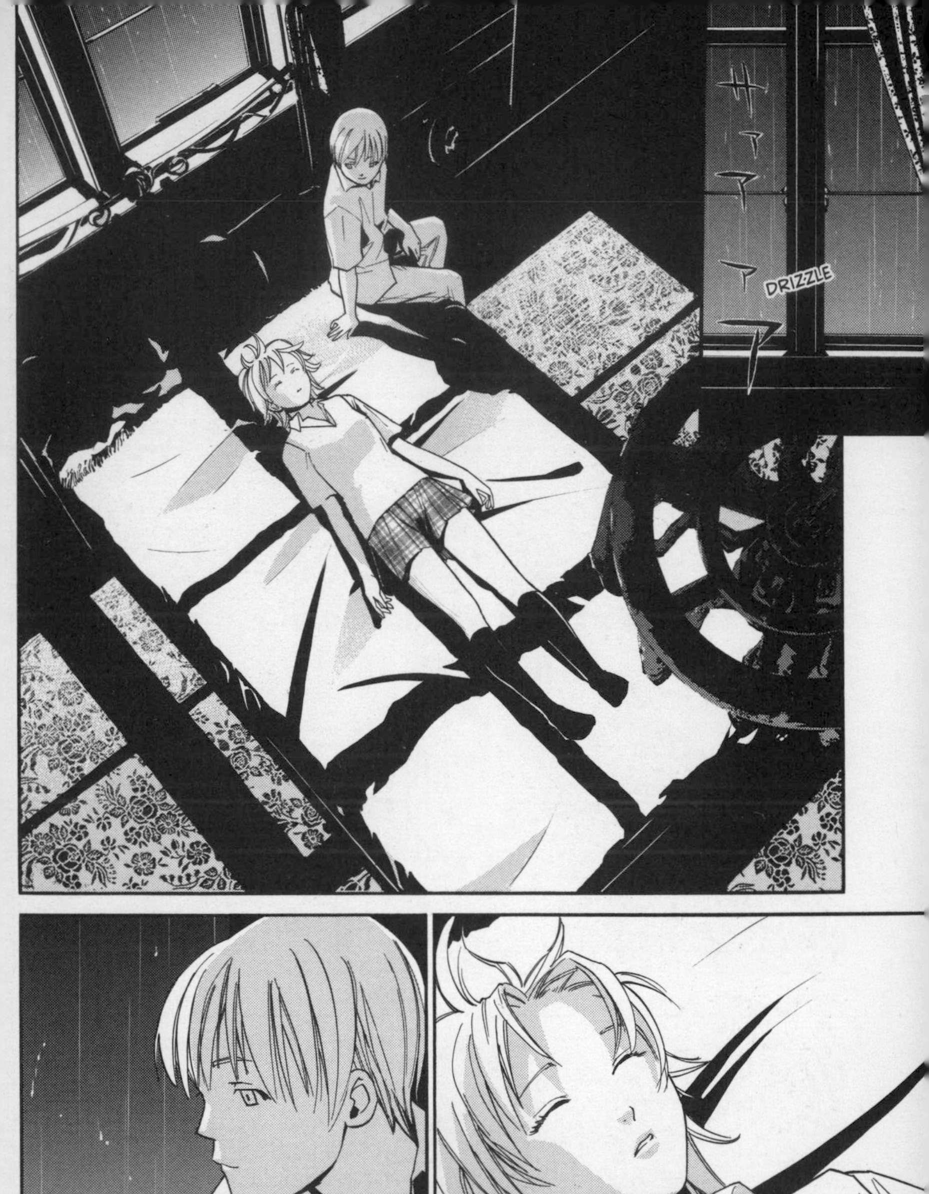
サァァァァ
DRIZZLE

WHY ARE YOU KEEPING SCUM LIKE THAT AROUND?
YOU AND TAISUKE ARE SO WEIRD.

YURA... WHEN YOU MET KANOU-KUN...
DID YOU KILL HIM?
OH? CURIOUS?

HE RETALIATED! HE'S STARTING TO REALIZE HIS "POWERS."
WATCH OUT, HE MIGHT SURPASS YOU, HIROSE!

OH MY...
YURA-KUN IS TOO RECKLESS... HE NEEDS TO BE MORE CAREFUL.

HIROSE-KUN, YOU'RE USUALLY LEVEL-HEADED, BUT YOU GET SO EMOTIONAL ABOUT KANOU-KUN.
...LET ME ASK YOU THIS.

IF HE EVER BECOMES AN OBSTACLE FOR US...
SHOULD WE JUST WARN HIM...
OR -

GO AHEAD.
KILL HIM.

VROOM
VROOOMM
NOBODY'S STOPPING...
NO, NO!
CAN'T GIVE UP NOW!!
POKE
SCREECH
VROOM

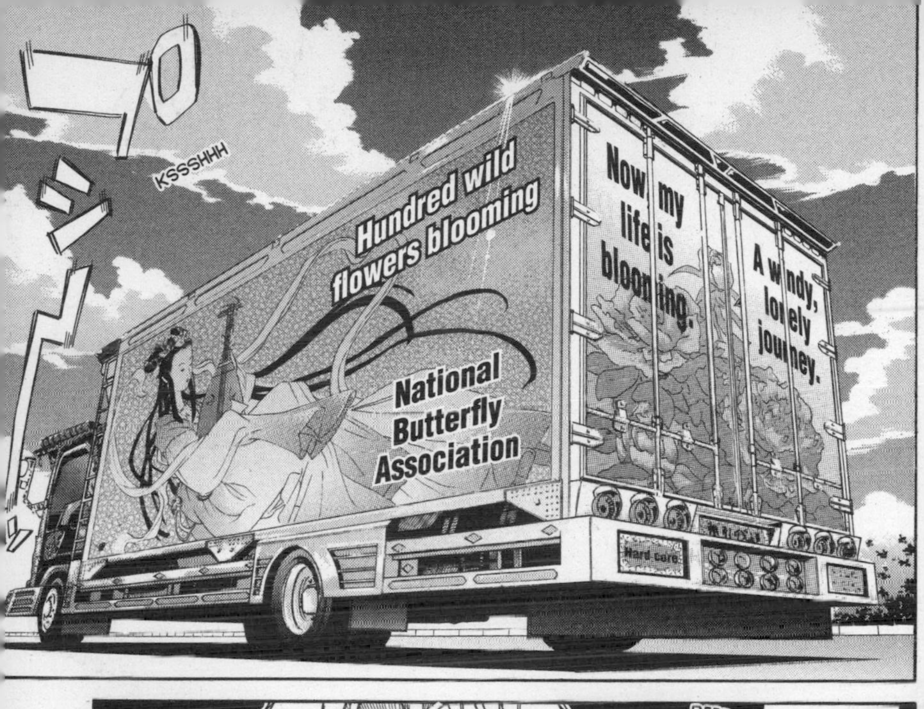
KSSSHHH
Hundred wild flowers blooming
National Butterfly Association
Now, my life is blooming.
A windy, lonely journey.
Hard core

BEEP
BEEP

BEEP
BEEP
VROOM
GRIT
....!!!
VWEEM
National Butterfly Association

POKE
ヒョコッ
WHAT'S THAT?
National Butterfly Association

HUH? OH!

BOING
THIS MORNING, I NOTICED THAT SOMEONE PULLED A PRANK ON MY BICYCLE...

SO I WAS HITCHHIK...
THAT'S NOT WHAT I MEANT.

WHAT DO YOU MEAN BY "NORTH"?
North

THAT'S...
North
WHERE I'M TRYING TO GO...

HMMMM...

G-CHAK
SIMPLE! I LIKE IT!
!
North
HOP IN.
I'M RYOU. WHAT'S YOUR NAME?
TA... TAISUKE KANOU...

National Battery Association
No help needed
ゴオオオ
VROOOM
SO, TAISUKE.
ジャラーン
JINGLE
ジャラーン
JINGLE

YOU'RE A STUDENT, RIGHT? RUNNING AWAY FROM HOME?
DON'T TELL ME YOU'RE WANDERING ABOUT LIKE A LONE WOLF?
...BUT WAIT, YOU HAVE A DESTINATION...
AHAHA, SOMETHING LIKE THAT!

FOR REAL?

......
WELL...
THEY SAY TABI WA MICHIZURE.
A windy, lonely journey.
Now, my life is blooming.
VROOM

BUMP

THIS IS A TRUCK STOP. I COME HERE OFTEN TO EAT AND TAKE NAPS...
GET OFF.
AND TAKE DOWN YOUR BICYCLE, TOO.

HEY THERE.
HEY, RYOU!

HEY, COULD YOU FIX THIS BICYCLE REAL QUICK?
HUH? WHY?

AND ADD SOME GEAR TO IT FOR LONG TRIPS.
Owwie....
Gotcha!
HUH?!

SNIFF SNIFF
DON'T WORRY, JUST COME WITH ME.

BUMP

OH, SORRY!

ARE YOU ALL RIGHT?

RYOU-SAN, I DIDN'T ASK FOR GEAR...!
DON'T WORRY ABOUT IT.

ガラッ
GRRRRM
WELCOME!

?
SIT.

OH, I DON'T NEED TO EAT.

...WHY?

UMM, BECAUSE I'M ON A DIET?
SIT DOWN.

TWO KATSUDON, PLEASE.

JEEET..
JEEET

......
HEY, TAISUKE.
DIG

WHAT DOES THIS LOOK LIKE?
POKE

??...
A... FATHER AND DAUGHTER...?
!?

THIS
IS MY DARLING AND CUTE LITTLE GIRL, ALMOST THREE YEARS OLD. ♡

AREN'T THEY SO ADORABLE? ♡

DON'T YOU DARE MENTION THIS TO THE GUYS OUTSIDE.
CLAP
I- I WON'T!!
...BUT WHY'D YOU SHARE IT WITH ME?

THINK OF IT THIS WAY.

SOMETIMES, IT'S EASIER TO TALK TO COMPLETE STRANGERS THAN YOUR FRIENDS ABOUT YOUR PROBLEMS...
BECAUSE YOU HAVE NOTHING TO LOSE.

SO TELL ME.
WHAT'S BOTHERING YOU?

UNBELIEVABLE, ISN'T IT?

HMM...
BUT THERE REALLY WERE MASS SUICIDES AND MYSTERIOUS DEATHS...

AND THERE'S NO REASON YOU'D LIE TO ME, TAISUKE...

ARE YOU WORRIED ABOUT YOUR TWO FRIENDS?

OF COURSE.
BUT...
WHAT CAN I DO?

TAISUKE...
THERE ARE THREE THINGS YOU CAN DO.

GO NORTH.
SLEEP.

AND EAT.

HERE YOU GO!
THUMP

CLINK
HAHA.
I GUESS THAT'S ALL I CAN DO...

FOR NOW.

ITADAKIMASU.
SNAP
パキ
パキ
SNAP

THIS PROBABLY MARKED...
ITADAKIMASU!

THE START OF MY LONG JOURNEY.

SPARKLE
SPARKLE

A-ARE YOU SURE ABOUT THIS?!
NO WORRIES. THEY OWE ME A LOT FROM MAHJONG BETS ANYWAY.

RYO-RYOU-SAN!
THANK YOU SO...

JINGLE
STUPID, THANK THOSE GUYS INSTEAD.
WE'RE LEAVING IN FIVE MINUTES.

DON'T FALL FOR HER...

JINGLE
JINGLE
チャリン
チャリン

ROAR

?

......

タッ
TROT

......

WHAT'S WRONG, RYOU?

FOR SOME REASON...
I CAN'T SEEM TO GET THROUGH.

WHAT?
HERE, YOU TRY, TOO.

TROT
TROT
TROT

...YOU'RE RIGHT!
SEE?
OH?

WHAT'S WRONG?

COMMOTION
ザワ
ザワ

WHAT'S WRONG?
HM? WE CAN'T GET THROUGH.

IT'S LIKE AN INVISIBLE WALL OR SOMETHING...
BUT I CAN'T FEEL IT...

WATCH.

FLING

ISN'T IT WEIRD? THE ROCK FALLS IN MID-AIR.
BOINK

SWING
HMPH!

...IT DOESN'T HURT...

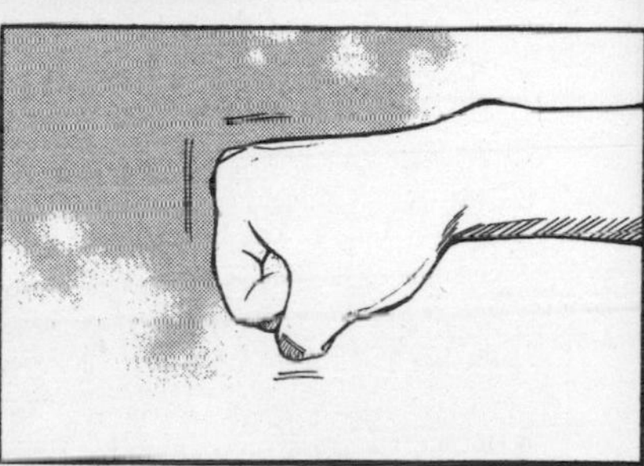

National Butterfly Association

...WHAT....?!
HEY, WHAT'S GOING ON HERE?

WHAT IS THIS FEELING...?
...DON'T TELL ME
TURN

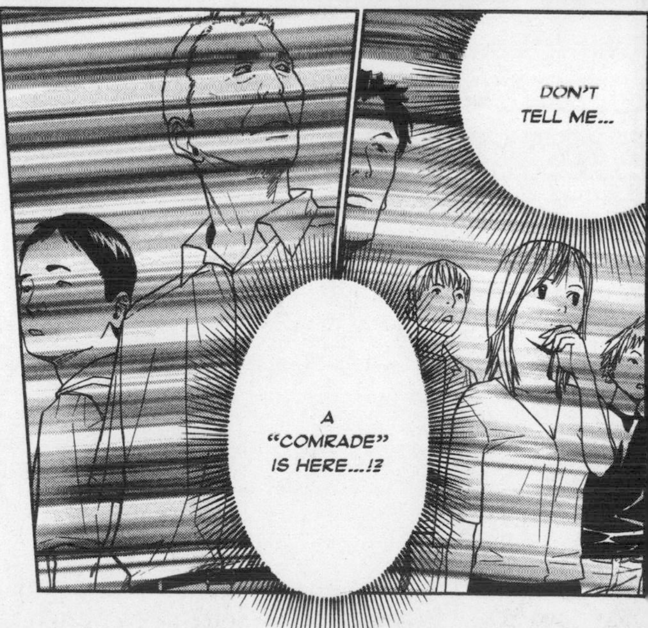
DON'T TELL ME...
A "COMRADE" IS HERE...!?
...OVER HERE.

National Butterfly Association

BUDDY, YOU'RE TOO SLOW. DIDN'T YOU NOTICE THAT I'M A "COMRADE"?
OH WELL.

I'M YUTA.

WHAT'S YOUR NAME, BUDDY?
WHAT POWERS DO YOU HAVE?

THI...

THIS BOY...!
Chapter 5/ End

Alive

The Final Evolution

I LEFT HOME TO GO FIND MEGU AND HIRO...
AND A TRUCK DRIVER, RYOU, BROUGHT ME TO THIS TRUCK STOP, BUT...
BUDDY, YOU'RE TOO SLOW. DIDN'T YOU NOTICE THAT I'M A "COMRADE"?
RYOU! THIS DRIVE-IN RESTAURANT SEEMS TO BE SURROUNDED BY A BARRIER!
OH GOSH... DON'T TELL ME...
I'M YUTA.
WHAT'S YOUR NAME, BUDDY? WHAT POWERS DO YOU HAVE?
WE'RE TRAPPED!?

Chapter 6
Here, Forever...
Live well. It is the greatest protest.

What is this!?
COMMOTION
We can't get out!!

YOU... DID THIS...?
YUP. I DID IT.
ヒラ
FLUTTER
ヒラ
FLUTTER
LIKE THIS...

SHNNK
!?

FHHT

IT DISAP- PEARED...!?
DORK, IT DIDN'T DISAPPEAR.
I JUST ISOLATED IT.

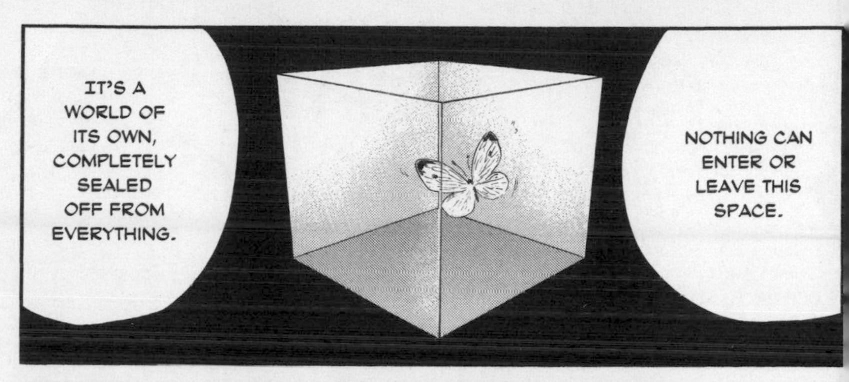
IT'S A WORLD OF ITS OWN, COMPLETELY SEALED OFF FROM EVERYTHING.
NOTHING CAN ENTER OR LEAVE THIS SPACE.

2-D Mart
THE SAME THING IS HAPPENING TO THIS DRIVE-IN RESTAURANT.

FROM THE OUTSIDE, THIS AREA LOOKS LIKE AN OPEN SPACE.
WHAT ...!?
NOW, I HAVE A QUESTION.

CLICK
CLICK
INSIDE THIS "BOX," CUT OFF FROM AIR AND ELECTRICITY...
?

AND SHUT OFF FROM ALL SIGNALS...

AND EVEN AIR...

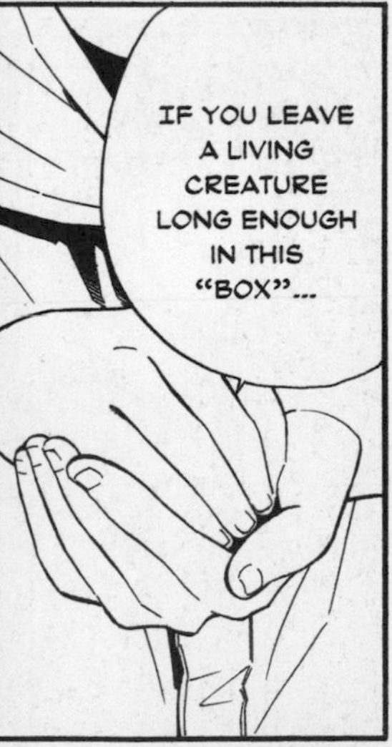
IF YOU LEAVE A LIVING CREATURE LONG ENOUGH IN THIS "BOX"...

WHAT DO YOU THINK WILL HAPPEN TO IT?

THIS BOY...

IS JUST LIKE HIRO AND THAT GUY...!!

...WHY ARE YOU DOING THIS...?!
BUDDY, AREN'T YOU A "COMRADE"?
DIDN'T YOU GET THE ORDER?

THE ORDER TO "DIE"...?

EVEN IF YOU'RE NOT AWARE OF IT...
DIDN'T YOU WANT TO DIE WHEN YOU SAW SOME-ONE ELSE DIE IN FRONT OF YOU?
I FELT IT WHEN I SAW MY MOTHER DIE.
I WAS ALMOST PULLED INTO IT...

WHUMP
AHH...

I'M SO JEALOUS...

COMMOTION
I'M JEALOUS OF DEATH...?

MY MOTHER DIED DURING THAT WEEK OF SUICIDES...
BUT SHE DIED SO PEACEFULLY.
THE REST OF THE PEOPLE HAVEN'T FIGURED IT OUT YET.

SO I'M GOING TO TEACH THEM...
ABOUT THE VALUE OF DEATH.

...YOU'RE WRONG.

GRIN
I DON'T WANT TO DIE.
AND I DON'T WANT TO SEE PEOPLE DYING.

I DON'T WANT ANYONE ELSE TO DIE...!

I'M GONNA FIND A WAY OUT OF THIS...!

プルプル
PUSH
PUSH
HAHA! LOOKS LIKE YOUR POWERS ARE USE-LESS AGAINST MINE, BUDDY.
TOTAL WIMP!
...URG.
THERE'S ONE WAY TO UNDO THIS ISOLATION, BUDDY...
JUST KILL ME.

TAISUKE!
MY CELL PHONE AND THE PAY PHONE IN THERE DON'T WORK.
OH? YOU'RE THE KID I BUMPED INTO EARLIER.
RYOU-SAN...
WHAT'S WRONG?
TOUCH
!

STOP IT!!
Whoa.
SWING
SLAP

HM?

HUH!?
ひっ
SNIFF

HE HIT ME!!
WHA.. WHAT ARE YOU DOING!?
S-SORRY!!
What's going on?
WAAAAAH
BUT...

RYOU-SAN, HE...
HE'S...!
WAAAAAH

WHIMPER
N- NEVER MIND.
EVEN IF I CLAIMED HE WAS THE CULPRIT...
NO ONE WOULD EVER BELIEVE ME.

SNEER

TH...
THAT BRAT...!!
Not fair!!

OH HEY, USELESS BUDDY.
WHAT!?
LET'S PLAY A GAME.

THERE'S ONLY ABOUT FOUR HOURS WORTH OF AIR IN HERE.
I WON'T DO ANYTHING ELSE...
SO IF YOU CAN BREAK THIS BARRIER, IT'S YOUR WIN, BUDDY.

IF YOU DON'T, IT'S GAME OVER.
OR, YOU CAN TRY A SIMPLER SOLUTION...
JUST KILL ME.

HEH!
ROLL
YOU'RE ON, PUNK!
I'LL BREAK THIS BARRIER IN NO TIME!
What's this about?
WHATEVER...!

MOM! LET'S IGNORE THAT DORK AND GO OVER THERE!
??
Useless wimpy dork...!
I'LL MAKE YOU CRY, KID!!

WAIT... THAT KID...
CALLED RYOU... "MOM"...?

IT'S ALREADY THREE HOURS...
THE SUN AND CLOUDS HAVEN'T MOVED AN INCH...
Japanese Restaurant Uki–
HFF
はぁ
HFF
IT'S LIKE A DIFFERENT WORLD IN HERE...

I'M THIRSTY...
IT'S SUFFOCATING...

はぁ
HFF
HFF
はぁ…
GLANCE
TICK
TOCK
JUST ONE MORE HOUR...

We Have Shaved Ice

GASP
はぁ

MISS.

GASP
はぁ
SIGH
ふう
YUTA...
I WAS WONDERING WHERE YOU WERE...
WHAT DO YOU HAVE...?

I RAN BY TO MY HOUSE AROUND THE CORNER...
Hah!
- ERR, I MEANT I HAD THIS ALL ALONG! HERE!!
...HM?
DON'T YOU NEED A DRINK, TOO, YUTA?
I'LL BE FINE! I'M A GENTLEMAN!
I FEEL BETTER ALL OF A SUDDEN...
HAHA! WELL, IF THAT'S THE CASE, I'LL HAVE SOME.
THANKS.

...ARE YOU HERE BY YOURSELF, YUTA?
YUP!
MOM AND I USED TO COME HERE OFTEN.
LOOK OVER THERE.

YOU SEE THAT DENT IN THE FENCE?
HM? OH YEAH...

MY MOM DID THAT.

MOM WAS A BAD DRIVER, SO SHE ALWAYS PRACTICED IN THIS PARKING LOT...
BUT SHE KEPT CRASHING.

THE RESTAURANT OWNERS ALWAYS CHEWED US OUT...

BUT IT WAS REALLY FUN.

THAT'S WHY...
I LIKE THIS PLACE.
ME, TOO.
I LIKE THE FOOD HERE.
TH-THEN, WILL YOU STAY WITH-
THUNK

HFF
はぁ
HFF
はぁ
...YOU'RE RUNNING OUT OF TIME.
...I KNOW!
THUNK

DIG
DIG
HAHA.
WHAT'S HE DOING?
DIG
DIG

OH...
THAT'S RIGHT.
I TOLD TAISUKE...
"DO ALL YOU CAN FOR NOW."
HE'S TRYING TO GO NORTH.
HFF
HFF
AND I NEED TO FIND A WAY TO RETURN TO MY FAMILY!
TIP
SPLASH
TROT
TROT
TROT

HEY! GET UP, YOU WIMPS!
WE NEED TO FIND A WAY OUT.
WHEEZE
ぜー、
GASP
はー、
WHEEZE
ぜー、
IT'S IMPOSSIBLE... EVEN A KNIFE DOESN'T WORK.
PANT
はー、

YOINK
ぐいぐい
DON'T GIVE UP!
Erk
WAAAH...
CLANK
カシャン

VWOOOM

IT'S HOPELESS...
HUH?
TIP
WHUMP
WHOA!

H-HUH? SUNSET ALREADY...?

H-HEY!
WE... WE CAN GET OUT!

WE'RE FREE!
ALL RIGHT!

ALL RIGHT! RYOU...

ALL RIGHT! YIPPEE!!

I FREED THEM.
SO GO AWAY.

WHERE'S RYOU-SAN?

JUST LEAVE!

......
CLUNK

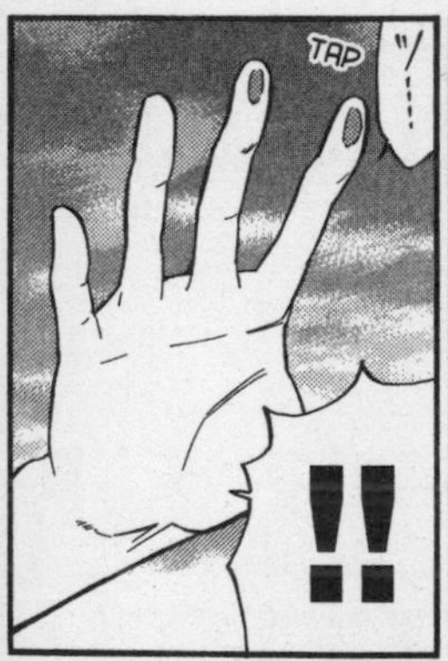
TAP
!!

YOU LOCKED HER INSIDE!?

...IT'S YOUR FAULT, TAISUKE
BECAUSE YOU DIDN'T KILL ME.
YOU BETTER KILL ME.
...OR ELSE, SHE'LL DIE.

URG!
YOU MAKE NO SENSE!!
WHY YOU...!
YOU TRY TO KILL EVERYONE BUT RELEASE THEM, AND ASK ME TO KILL YOU BUT THEN YOU TELL ME TO GO AWAY!!

AND NOW, YOU LOCKED IN RYOU-SAN -
Hah!

OH WAIT... YOU...
YOU WANT...
RYOU-SAN TO STAY WITH YOU?

NO...
THEN WHY DID YOU GIVE HER FOOD AND DRINK?!

YOU WOULDN'T FEED SOMEONE IF YOU'RE GONNA KILL THEM!

...AND YOU CALLED RYOU-SAN...
"MOM"...!

NO...
YOU KNOW... YOU'RE ONLY A LITTLE BOY, AFTER ALL...
YOU ISOLATED EVERYONE, NOT TO KILL THEM, BUT...
JUST SO THAT YOU COULD BE WITH RYOU-SAN IN PLACE OF YOUR "MOM"!!
NO!

I...
I...
I WAS ORDERED TO "DIE"...!
THAT'S WHY... I NEED TO DIE...!

SO KILL ME NOW!

WHAT... THE HECK...
CHOOSE NOW!!
YOU CAN EITHER KILL ME OR WATCH HER DIE!
MAKE YOUR CHOICE...
I WON'T DO ANY OF THAT!

I'LL FIGURE SOMETHING OUT!!
I...
I...

HRK...
GRIT

IF...
AT A TIME LIKE THIS...

I REALLY HAVE POWERS...
THEN I NEED TO...
USE THEM NOW!!
SHNNK...
ジャキン…

SPURT

CLUNK
カタ…
...I RECEIVED THE ORDER JUST NOW.
DID YOU RECEIVE IT TOO, YUTA?
YUTA, WHICH WOULD YOU CHOOSE?
"LIFE" OR "DEATH"?
SPURT

I...
I...
タ...
DRIP
ポタ
DRIP

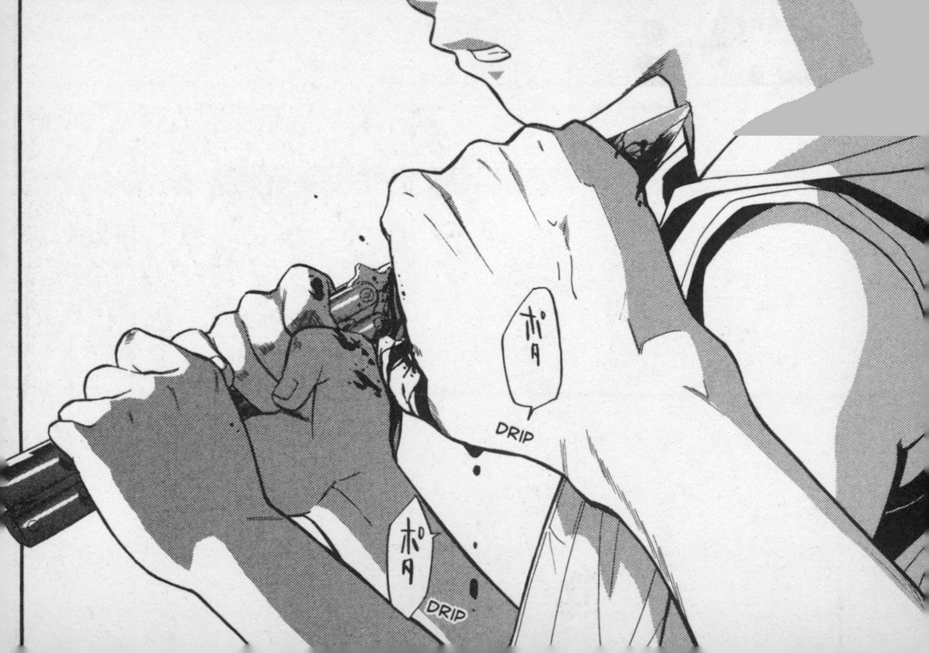
ポタ
DRIP
ポタ
DRIP

HFF
PANT
GASP

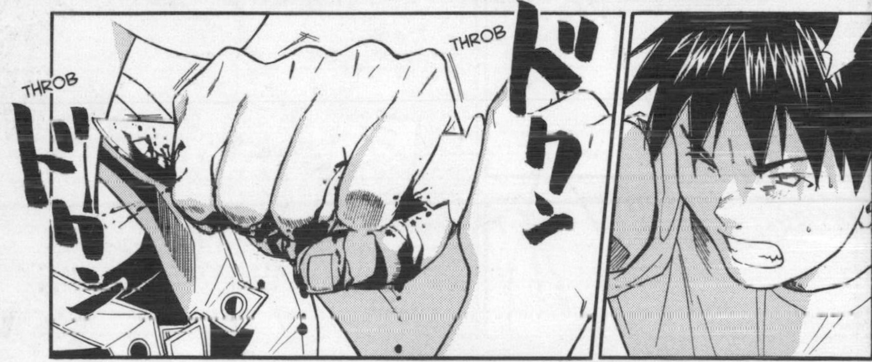
THROB
THROB

...YOU DON'T WANT TO DIE, RIGHT?

MOMMY!
MOMMY!!

WAAAAAAAH!

OH...
SO HE LOCKED ME IN BECAUSE I LOOKED LIKE HIS MOTHER...

YEAH... SO...
HAHA. IT'S OKAY. I'M NOT MAD.

BUT, PEOPLE WITH STRANGE POWERS...
REALLY EXIST, DON'T THEY?

EVEN HIM, THOUGH HE SLEEPS LIKE AN ANGEL.

STRANGE POWERS, HUH...

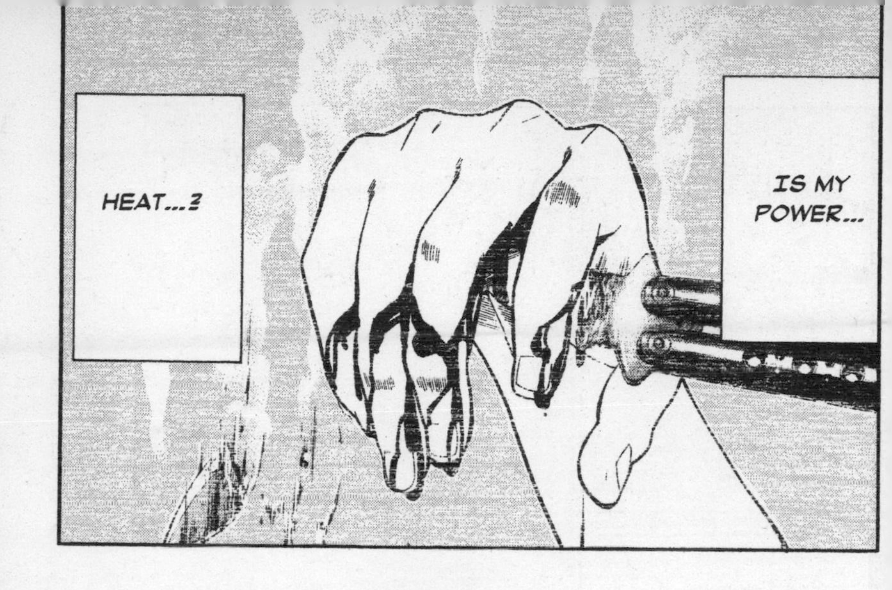
IS MY POWER...
HEAT...?

MMM...

CHIRP
CHIRP
GRRRM

OH, GOOD MORNING.

SORRY, YUTA! RYOU-SAN LEFT ALREADY.

SHE WAS WORRIED ABOUT YOU, BUT SHE HAD TO RETURN TO HER FAMILY...
RUSTLE
BUT, SHE LEFT YOU THIS NOTE.

TEL. 090-119
If you ever feel lonely, call me.
I'll give you a ride on my big truck next time.
Ryou

...GEE, SHE LEFT BEFORE I COULD APOLOGIZE TO HER.
WHAT ARE YOU STILL DOING HERE, TAISUKE?

UMM, I WAS WAITING FOR SOMEONE.
WHO?

YOU.

HOP ON. I'LL TAKE YOU HOME.

OH...
SO...YOU WERE WAITING FOR ME...

...MY HOME IS REALLY FAR.
WHERE IS IT?

Chapter 6/ End

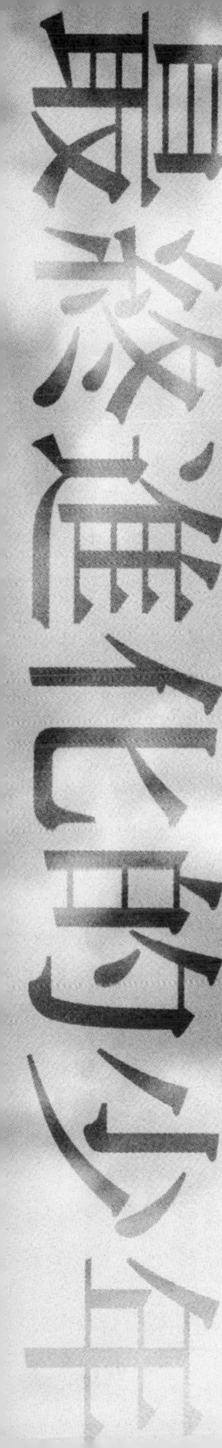
最終進化的少年

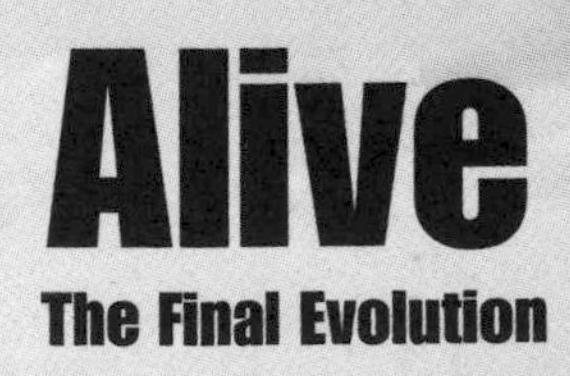
Alive
The Final Evolution

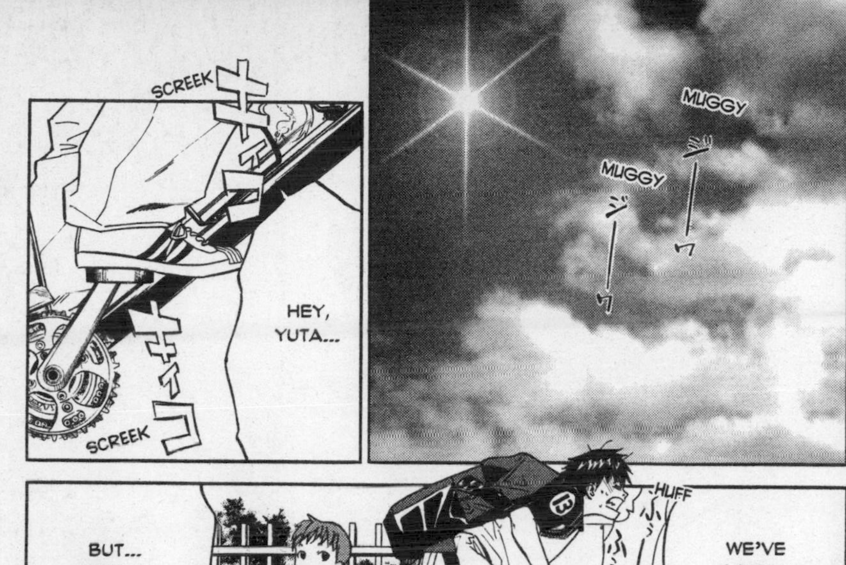
MUGGY
MUGGY
SCREEK
HEY, YUTA...
SCREEK

HUFF
WE'VE GOTTEN PRETTY FAR...
GRUNT
BUT... WHERE IS YOUR HOUSE?
SCREEK
SCREEK

WE PASSED IT A LONG TIME AGO.
ABOUT TWO HOURS BACK.
BRAKE

YOU TRICKED ME?!
Chapter 7
For What?
Men are not against you, they are merely for themselves.

THIS KID IS YUTA TAKIZAWA.
COOL!
HE'S A THIRD-GRADE BRAT.

BUT HE'S NO ORDINARY BRAT.
HE HAS STRANGE POWERS LIKE HIROSE AND HIS "COMRADES."
VWOOOM

HIS POWER IS "ISOLATION."

HE HAS THE POWER TO ISOLATE AN AREA, SEPARATING IT FROM THE OUTSIDE WORLD.

IN FACT, HE ISOLATED THE WHOLE DRIVE-IN RESTAURANT AREA AND TRAPPED EVERYONE INSIDE IT.

BUT...
IT WAS JUST A CHILDISH TANTRUM TO AVOID LONELINESS...
HEY, TAISUKE, NORTH IS THAT WAY.
SHUT UP!!

WHEN I SAID TO GO NORTH, I MEANT THAT I WANTED TO TRAVEL WITH YOU. DIDN'T YOU GET IT?
...SHUT UP!!
GLIDE

DON'T BE MAD! I'LL HELP YOU FIND MEGU AND HIRO.
WE SHOULD GET ALONG, "COMRADE."

WHA....!?

NO WAY!!

KNOCK
KNOCK
G-CHAK
OCHIAI-SAN.
CREAK
HOW ARE YOU FEELING?

I FEEL BAD FOR LOCKING YOU UP...
...THEN LET ME GO, HIROSE-KUN.

WHY DO YOU LOCK ME UP?! WHERE ARE WE?!
LET ME GO HOME!!

I'M GLAD YOU FEEL BETTER, BUT...
CLUNK
WHERE'S TAISUKE?!
TAISUKE FELL OFF THE ROOF, TOO!!
IS HE OKAY?!
...OCHIAI-SAN

I...
I WAS GIVEN AN IMPORTANT MISSION.
I WANT YOU TO SEE ME COMPLETE IT.
WHERE IS TAISUKE!?
...I'LL LEAVE YOUR FOOD HERE.
G-CHAK
BAM
HIRO...
G-CHAK

BANG
HIROSE-KUN!
BANG
HIROSE-KUN!
- WAY...
HE'S IN THE WAY...

TAISUKE IS IN THE WAY.
IN THE WAY...

...HE'S SO UNSTABLE.
MAYBE WE SHOULD GET RID OF KANOU-KUN SOON...

HUH?
CAMPING!?
THUNK
THUNK
YOU DIDN'T TELL ME ABOUT THIS!!
WHAT ELSE CAN WE DO? WE'RE LOST!!

WHAT ABOUT A BATH?! AND A CHANGE OF CLOTHES?!
...WE'LL GO WITHOUT IT TONIGHT.
WHAAAT!?

WHAT ABOUT FOOD?!
Hahaha
WE'LL COOK FISH! GOTTA CATCH THEM FIRST, THOUGH!
SO HELP ME OUT!

Awwww
I HATE FISH! I HATE TOUCHING IT, TOO!!
Boo Boo
WHATEVER!

SPLASH
SPLASH

OOFS!
SPLASH
AWW, IT GOT AWAY!
SPLASH

BUT THIS IS SO FUN...
Ahaha
GIGGLE
AND THE WATER IS SO NICE AND COOL ♡

I-I'LL DO IT, TOO!
GRIN
Heh
DUMB-ASS...

WHAT'S HE DOING...?

!

SHHK

SPLASH
OKAY! I GOT ONE!!

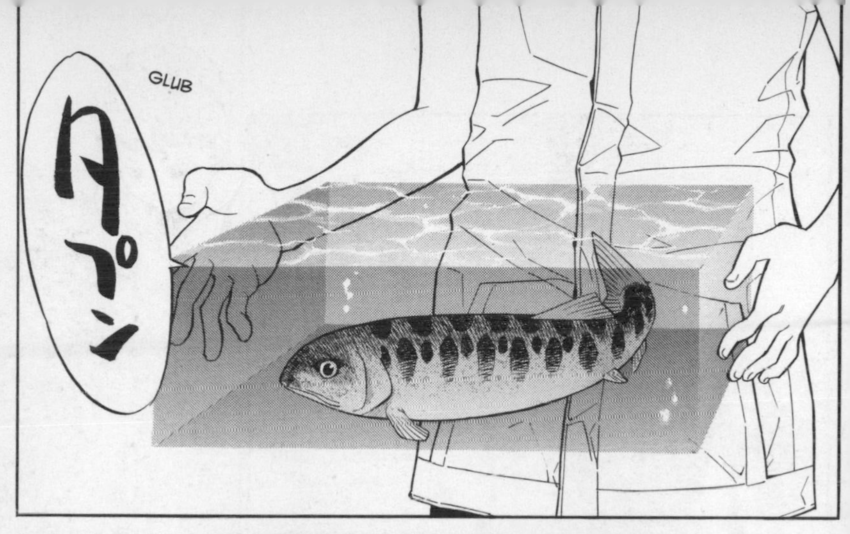
GLUB
タプン

SNEER
ニヤリ

......
SPLASH
ドシャン
バッシャン
SPLASH!
DUMBASS...
ザブ
GLUB
ザブ
GLUB

YOU ALSO FORGOT A LIGHTER?!
YOU CAN'T FIND YOUR WAY AROUND, AND CAN'T EVEN FISH. YOU'RE SO USELESS...!
WHERE IS IT?!

......
OH YEAH!

HEY, TAISUKE, LIGHT IT YOURSELF.
HUH?
YOU MELTED A KNIFE YESTERDAY.
YOU MIGHT BE ABLE TO START A FIRE WITH ALL THAT HEAT.

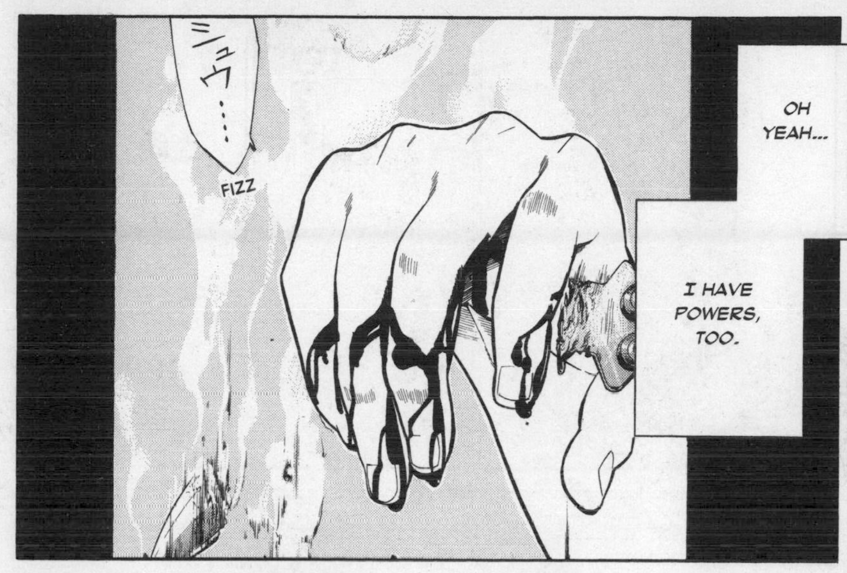
OH YEAH...
I HAVE POWERS, TOO.
シュウ…
FIZZ

IF YOU CAN'T START A FIRE, I'LL DEMOTE YOU TO WANSUKE.
ホレ
Fetch!
Wan...?
WANSUKE

JUST WATCH, YOU STUPID BRAT!
GRAB

HERE WE GO!

HUMPH!
SNAP

...THE BRANCH IS TOO THIN.
ONCE MORE!

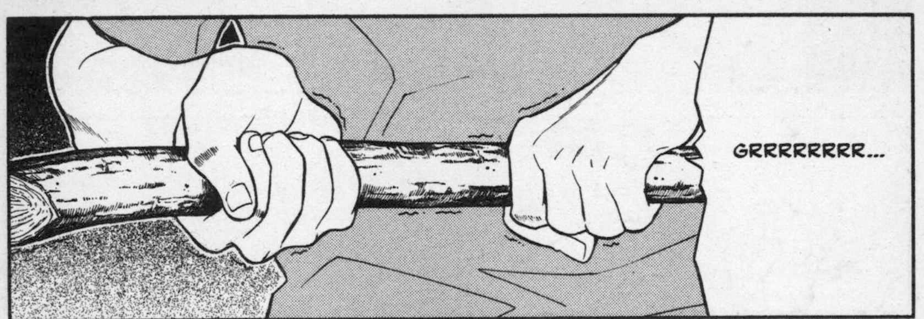
GRRRRRRRR...

C'MON....!

SIGH.
SILENCE

WHY?! WHY CAN'T I DO IT?!
DON'T DEMOTE ME TO WANSUKE!
HEY.

YOU'RE JUST TENSING UP.
YOU NEED TO FULLY UNDERSTAND YOUR POWER AND VISUALIZE ITS EFFECT.

He talks smart...
...SO HOW DO I DO THAT?
EH?
YOU MEAN... YOU USED YOUR POWER SUBCON-SCIOUSLY?
YOU'RE WEIRD...

THE BASIS OF MY POWER IS "BOXING" THINGS...
SO I VISUALIZE A BOX...
TAISUKE, YOUR POWER IS PROBABLY "HEAT," SO YOU SHOULD VISUALIZE A FIRE.
SIT, CLOSE YOUR EYES, AND CONCENTRATE!
......

MY POWER IS "HEAT."

IF MY POWERS CAME OUT OF MY HAND...

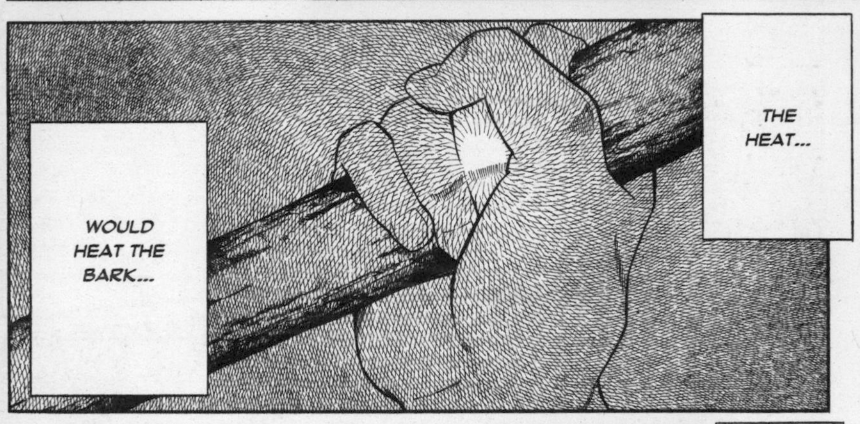
THE HEAT...
WOULD HEAT THE BARK...

AND BURST INTO A FLAME.

FZZ...

FZZZ...

ポンポン PAT PAT
KEEP CONCENTRATING YOUR POWER INTO YOUR HAND...
AND VISUALIZE IT IN YOUR HEAD, RIGHT HERE.

FOR EXAMPLE...
A FLAME AT THE END OF THE BRANCH...
A SMALL...
FLAME.

BOOF
WHOA!?

THAT'S HOW I MASTERED MY "ISOLATION" POWER.
NOW LET'S HURRY UP AND COOK DINNER.
BURN BURN

YOUHEIDO
PUBLICATIONS
IN TOKYO

Mystery of the Mass Suicides Part 3

Mass Suicides

Were a Precursor to Geologic Catastrophe!

Lemming phenomena?

The hidden human extinction

This week an epidemic of suicides claimed victims all over the world for reasons still unknown.

But Michio Abe, a former scientist at the Disaster Prevention Science Lab, gave a statement.

“Organisms exhibit abnormal behaviors in response to major magnetic shifts. Humans, after all, are organisms too, so it could be assumed that they were affected by changes in the Earth, too.”

Beached whales and herds of lemming jumping into the sea could be seen as mass suicides, also.

These behaviors are borne from environmental stresses and external causes which might induce mass hysteria.

“Usuall[illegible] Abe con[illegible]

“This [illegible] never occurred before. Advancements in the living environment surpassed the pace of technological advancements, causing great changes. Maybe humans could not adjust fast enough to these rapid changes.” It could be possible that humans could not adapt well to the rapid changes so the brain panicked and it resulted in abnormal behavior. If so, what triggered it?

[illegible]ere [illegible]ple [illegible]ven to end their own lives? Theories like the Suicide Virus, etc. overlook the strange behavior of animals. A complete analysis from a fresh, new perspective.

AMAMIYA-KUN ♡
BONK
Dammit! Dammit!
BADUM
BONK
AMAMIYA'S AT IT AGAIN...
YOU SHOULDN'T TALK TO HER NOW...
Let's go.

AWW BUMMER, STRESSED OUT AGAIN, AMAMIYA-SAN?
CLOMP
CLOMP

DO YOU HAVE MENO-PAUSE?
CLOMP
CLOMP

...WELL, THERE'S REALLY NOTHING YOU CAN DO.
Oolong Tea
G-DUNK

OUR MAGAZINE HANDLES OCCULT FARCE...
SO WE'RE NOT TAKEN SERIOUSLY.
Enjoy Coca-Cola
coke
NOT YOU TOO, ODA-CHAN –

NIGHTMARE WEEK WAS A GLOBAL TRAGEDY!
I WANT TO WRITE A SERIOUS ARTICLE ABOUT IT!
I DIDN'T JOIN THIS COMPANY TO WRITE TRASHY ARTICLES LIKE THAT!
Ahaha
YEAH, YOUR LEMMING THEORY IS PRETTY FAR OUT.

HEY, THE SUI-CIDE VIRUS SEEMS MORE BELIEVABLE...
Whoah!
HOW CAN YOU SAY THAT?! THERE'S NO PROOF OF A VIRUS YET!
BESIDES, I THINK BOTH THEORIES ARE FAR-FETCHED ANYWAY!
BUT THIS CASE ISN'T OVER YET!

AFTER THAT STRING OF SUICIDES, MANY PEOPLE AROUND THE NATION WENT MISSING.
POLICE
POLICE
Police Station Slaughte
Dead
onnection to
At five o'clock on the 12th, a college student (21) discovered several police station employees lying down at the front information counter of the Tokyo
Central Police
AND THERE WERE ALWAYS STRANGE DEATHS LINKED TO MISSING PEOPLE.
he police
license, but
unconscious
the floor, and
sought help in the

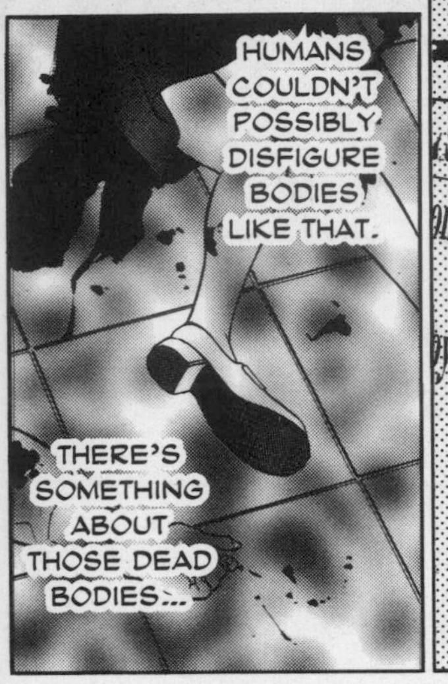
HUMANS COULDN'T POSSIBLY DISFIGURE BODIES LIKE THAT.
THERE'S SOMETHING ABOUT THOSE DEAD BODIES...

YOU MEAN... MASS SUICIDES, MISSING PEOPLE, AND STRANGE DEATHS ARE SOMEHOW CONNECTED?
GRAB
I DON'T KNOW...

BUT THERE IS A PLACE...
WHERE ALL THREE INCIDENTS OCCURRED.
AT A HIGH SCHOOL IN TOKYO... IF I CHECK THAT PLACE...

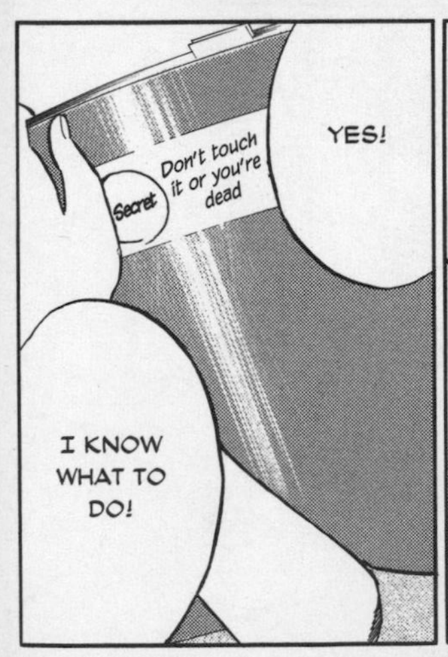
YES!
Secret
Don't touch it or you're dead
I KNOW WHAT TO DO!

I'VE DECIDED! I'M GOING TO RE-INVESTIGATE THIS!
I'LL START WITH...

THIS BOY!!
Students questioned for the brutal high school Murders
Yuichi Hirose (16)
Boy H
i O. (16)
Missing
Taisuke Kanou (16)
Childhood Friend of both
Strange deaths of four high
and suicides of a male
Male teacher that

HMMMM...

TAISUKE, I'M GOING TO SLEEP...
OH, SURE...

HEY YUTA, WHY DO WE HAVE THESE POWERS?
DUNNO.

WHEN DID YOU GAIN YOUR POWER?
OH, IT WAS WHEN MY MOM DIED.

I just stepped on an
emotional land mine!
HEY, I'M ALL RIGHT.
I'VE THOUGHT ABOUT THIS A LOT MYSELF.

WHY DID MOM COMMIT SUICIDE?
WHY DID I GAIN THESE POWERS?
WHAT ENTERED OUR BODIES IN THE FIRST PLACE...?

WHUMP
"ENTERED"...?
– AH!
VZZ...
YEAH...!
THEN, I
SAW THE
UNIVERSE...
RIGHT
AFTER
THAT...
DIE.

WAS THAT
THE ORDER
TO "DIE"?
YEAH.
I THINK THE
PEOPLE WHO
DIED FOLLOWED
THAT ORDER.
LIKE MY
MOM.

"SOMETHING" CAME FROM SOMEWHERE AND ENTERED HUMAN BODIES...
AND ORDERED HUMANS TO DIE...
AND THOSE WHO DIDN'T COMPLY... BECAME "COMRADES"...
AND GAINED POWERS...

WHAT IS THIS POWER FOR...?

WHO KNOWS... BUT...
BUT YOU'RE KINDA SPECIAL, TAISUKE... BECAUSE YOU SEEM TO LACK A LOT OF THINGS.
COMPARED TO THE OTHERS, YOU'RE INCOMPLETE...

HAVE YOU MET OTHER "COMRADES," YUTA?
YEAH, JUST ONE.
BUT HE SAID SCARY STUFF LIKE "THE VALUE OF DEATH," SO I JUST IGNORED HIM.

SO YOU JUST REPEATED HIS STUFF AT THE DRIVE-IN RESTAURANT?
SO I'M GOING TO TEACH THEM...
OF COURSE.
ABOUT THE VALUE OF DEATH.

OH. I THOUGHT ALL THE "COMRADES" TALKED LIKE THAT...
I'LL GUIDE YOU TO THE PATH OF "DEATH."
BY THE WAY, WAS HE A CURLY-HAIRED GUY IN COVER-ALLS?
NO.
OH...
SO HOW DO YOU PICK OUT A "COMRADE"? WHAT'S THE TRICK?
HUH?

WAIT A MINUTE. YOU'RE TRYING TO FIND YOUR FRIENDS WHO ARE WITH "COMRADES" WITH-OUT KNOWING HOW TO PICK THEM OUT?
YEAH.
WITH THE ONLY CLUE, "NORTH"?
EXACTLY.
アオーン
AWOOOO

HOW RECK-LESS...
Wow, he's really dumb.
バカ
AWOOOO
?
YUTA?
OH, THE TRICK IS...
YOU SORT OF...
JUST SENSE IT...

......
...WHAT'S WRONG?

......
A "COMRADE" IS COMING.

DASH

WH- WHERE ARE WE GOING?!
HIDING!!
IF IT'S HIM AGAIN...

FLASH
HE'LL KILL ME FOR SURE!!

SCREEEECH
!

VROOM

......
YOU KNOW, THEY CAN SENSE US, TOO.

G-CHAK
GRIT

GOOD EVENING!

DID I SCARE YOU GUYS? I'M SORRY.
BAM

H-HUH?
IT'S NOT HIM...
HE SEEMS LIKE A NICE GUY. YOU SCARED ME.

I GOT LOST.
BUT I DIDN'T EXPECT TO FIND ANOTHER "COMRADE."
RUSTLE

GOOD EVENING, MISTER. IS THIS YOUR FIRST TIME MEETING ANOTHER "COMRADE"?
Hey...
NO, THAT'S NOT WHAT I MEANT.

I WASN'T TOLD THAT TAISUKE KANOU HAD ANOTHER "COMRADE" WITH HIM.
KATSUMATA-SAN DIDN'T MENTION THAT.
FWOOO
WHOOM

FWOOOOOOMMM
WHOA!?
VWOOOOOSH

WH-DOOM
FLAP
FLAP

RUSTLE
FLAP
FLAP
RUSTLE

URGH...
RUSTLE
RUSTLE
VWOOOOOSH
COUGH
COUGH

COUGH
COUGH
WHAT WAS THAT...?!

!
YU...

YUTA!!

YU...
ヒュオ
FWOOOM

FSAAAT

EE...!?

WH... WHAT!?

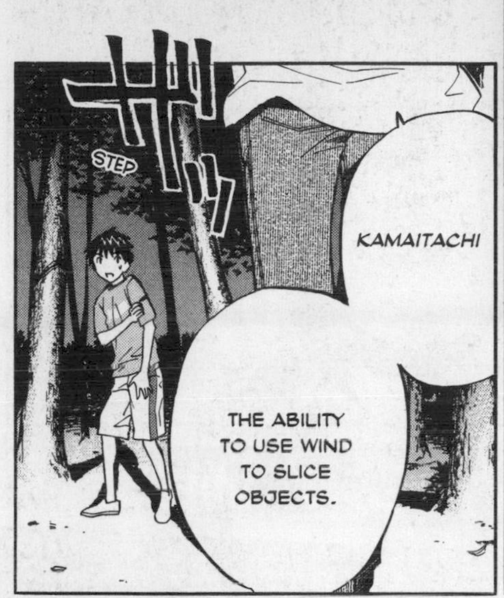
STEP
KAMAITACHI
THE ABILITY TO USE WIND TO SLICE OBJECTS.

STEP
NOW THAT YOU KNOW WHAT MY POWER IS.
LET'S BE FAIR AND TELL ME WHAT YOUR POWER IS.
STEP

FAIR, HUH...
THAT'S KIND OF HYPOCRITICAL TO ASK THAT AFTER YOU AMBUSH US...

OH, SORRY
BUT I THOUGHT TWO TO ONE WASN'T FAIR, EITHER.
STEP
STEP
KATSUMATA-SAN ASKED ME...
TO MAKE SURE YOU DIE.

STEP
NICE TO MEET YOU, TAISUKE KANOU.
I'M MORIO.
MY POWER IS "WIND."

SO,
SHALL WE BEGIN?
Continued in Volume 3

Light Visual Manga 2

SUDDENLY...

SINCE YOU'RE A RABBIT, YOUR NAME WILL BE...
"STEW"!!
WHAT!?
IT WAS AN UNAVOIDABLE NAME.

OH YEAH, I WENT TO BUY A DESK...
DROP
Pet food
I TOTALLY FORGOT.
HOP HOP

AND, PETS ARE PROHIBITED HERE...!!
Oh no...
AND I VIOLATED THE CONTRACT.
HOP HOP

PEEE...
Hah
POOP

RABBIT!!
GRAAAH!
I'LL MAKE STEW OUT OF YOU IF YOU MISBEHAVE!!!

LICK
LICK

OHH...
WOOOOW ♡
IN THE END, I WAS FOOLED BY ITS CUTENESS...

...SO, ARE YOU MALE OR FEMALE?
FUNNY TO VERBALLY ASK
AND NOW, IT'S NOT A PET, BUT FAMILY.

GO STEW! PART 1

GO STEW! PART 2

SLEEPING STEW

THANK YOU SO MUCH FOR READING ALL THIS!!

Alive

The Final Evolution

Translation Notes

Japanese is a tricky language for most Westerners, and translation is often more art than science. For your edification and reading pleasure, here are notes on some of the places where we could have gone in a different direction with our translation of the work, or where a Japanese cultural reference is used.

Tai-chan, Kattsun, pages 20, 32

Tai-chan is a nickname for Taisuke, and Kattsun is a nickname Yura made for Katsumata.

Tabi wa michizure, page 73

Tabi wa michizure is a Japanese saying that means "Fellow travelers help each other."

Katsudo, page 76

Katsudon is a pork cutlet bowl, a relatively cheap Japanese version of a fast food dish. The price is close to a McDonald's value meal.

Itadakimasu, page 83

Itadakimasu is a Japanese greeting said before meals meaning "Thank you for this meal."

Zaru soba, page 118

Zaru soba are cold *soba* (buckwheat noodles) served on a flat osier basket (zaru).

Wansuke, page 163

The first kanji character for "Taisuke" has a dot at the bottom. If the dot is placed at the top right corner, it becomes the kanji character for "dog." *Wansuke* is a slang term for "dog" or "doggie."

Kamaitachi, page 191

Kamaitachi is a mythical phenomenon in which winds mysteriously cut or slice people and objects like a *kama* (sickle). It was thought to be caused by an *itachi* (weasel), so the term *kamaitachi* (sickle weasel) came about.

You are going the wrong way!

Manga is a completely different type of reading experience.

To start at the *beginning*, go to the *end*!

That's right! Authentic manga is read the traditional Japanese way—from right to left. Exactly the opposite of how American books are read. It's easy to follow: Just go to the other end of the book, and read each page—and each panel—from right side to left side, starting at the top right. Now you're experiencing manga as it was meant to be.